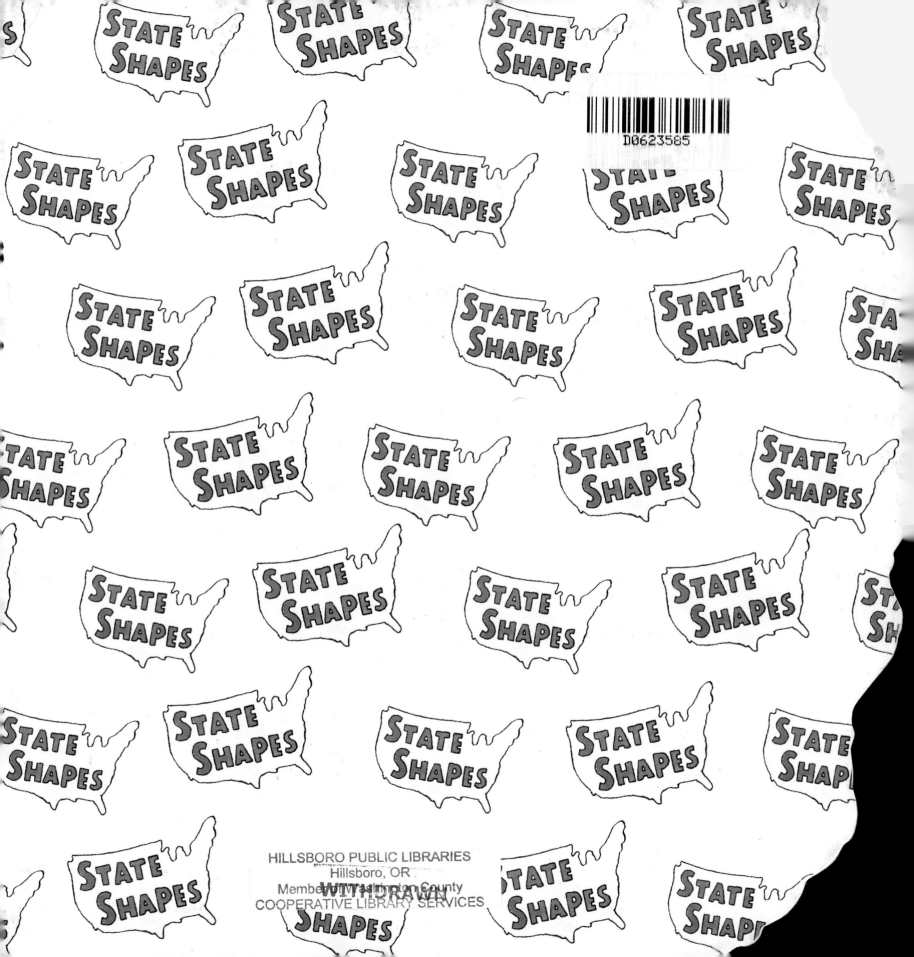

Published by
Black Dog & Leventhal Publishers, Inc.
151 West 19th Street
New York, NY 10011

Distributed by
Workman Publishing Company
708 Broadway
New York, NY 10003

Designed by 27.12 design, ltd.

Manufactured in Hong Kong

ISBN: 1-57912-101-2 *4261 6341 02/10*

h g f e d c b a

Library-of-Congress Cataloging-in-Publication Data

Bruun, Erik A., 1961-
Illinois / by Erik Bruun.
p. cm. -- (State Shapes)

Summary: Presents the history, important people, and famous places of Illinois,
as well as miscellaneous facts about the state today.

ISBN 1-57912-101-2
1. Illinois--Juvenile literature. [1. Illinois.] I. Title.

F541.3 .B78 2000

977.3--dc21   00-024686

ILLINOIS

BY ERIK BRUUN

illustrated by

RICK PETERSON

BLACK DOG
& LEVENTHAL
PUBLISHERS
NEW YORK

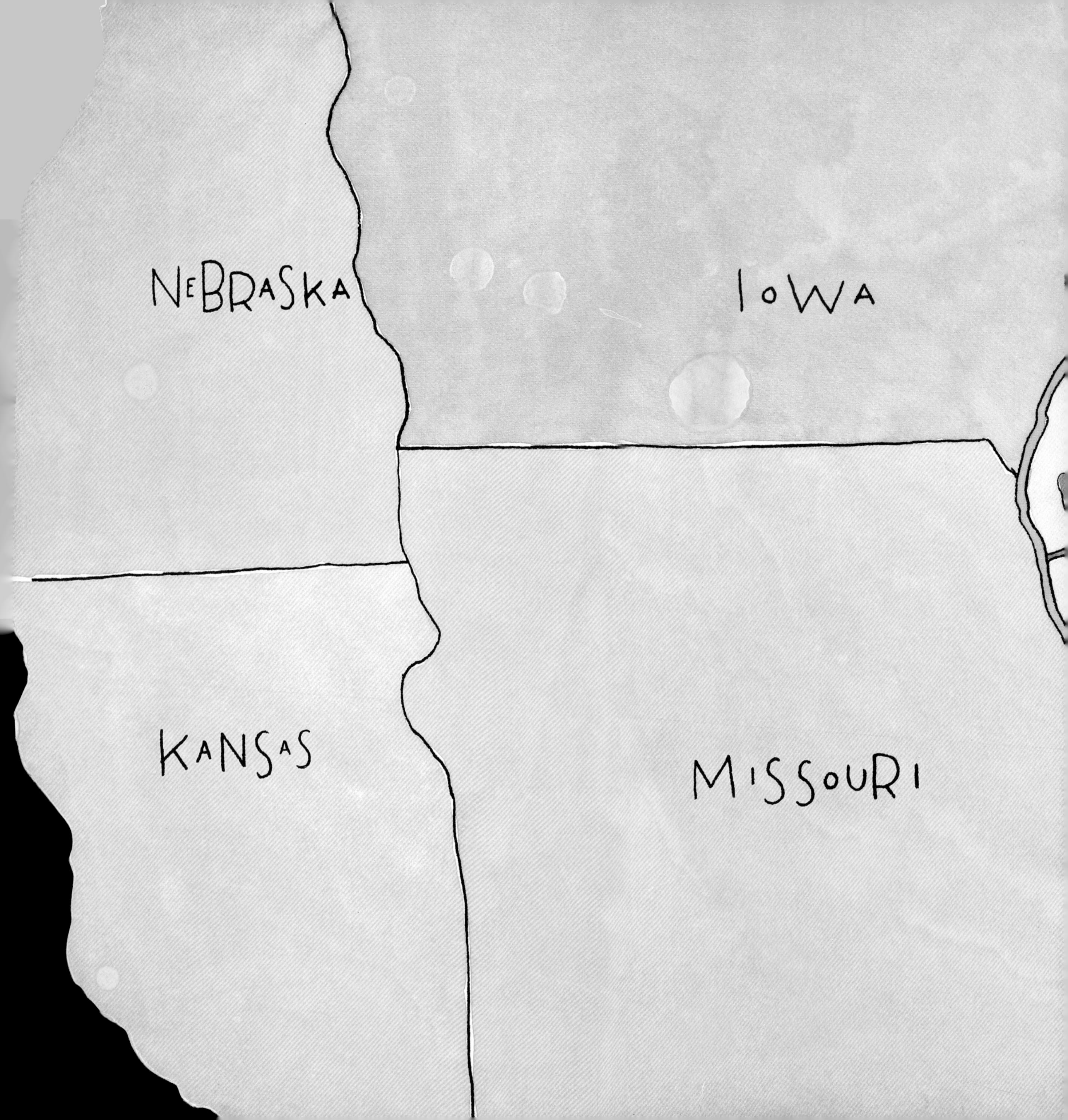
NEBRASKA
IOWA
KANSAS
MISSOURI

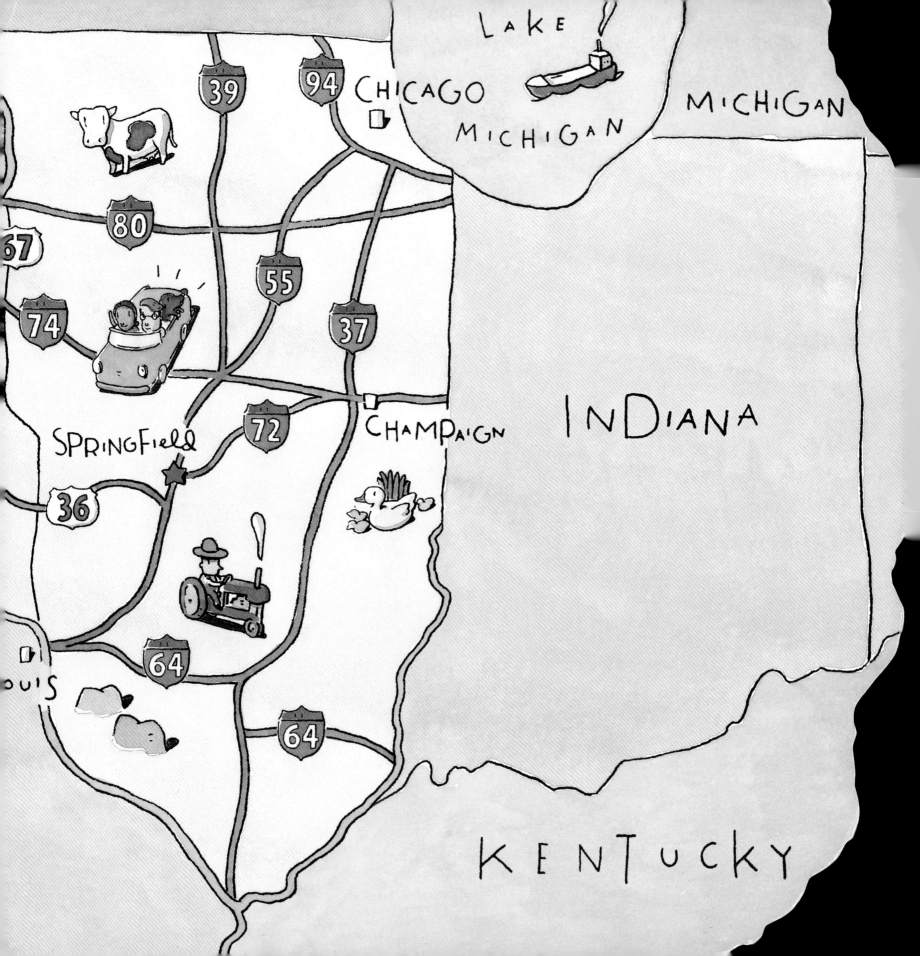

Welcome to Illinois! My name is Lorraine Hawkins. I will be taking you on a tour through the glorious state of Illinois—the Land of Lincoln, the Crossroads of America and the "Garden Spot of the Nation," right smack in America's heartland. We will see everything from the blustery Windy City of Chicago and the majestic, meandering Mississippi River to some of our country's most fertile farmland. It is a fascinating state, from top to bottom!

Great! My name's J.P. and this is my dog, Maggie. To start with, can you tell us why Illinois is called "The Tall State?"

For lot's of reasons. Abraham Lincoln, Illinois' most famous resident, was tall. Robert Wadlow, the world's tallest man, came from Illinois. Corn stalks are tall. The skyscrapers in Chicago are

Q. How did the town of Aledo, Illinois, get its name?

tall. Even the shape of the state itself is tall. If Illinois were on the East Coast, it would stretch from New York State to North Carolina.

Are you going to be telling me any tall tales?

Nope. You are going to hear some interesting and strange stories, but they will all be true! We will start our journey at perhaps the most mysterious place of all—the Cahokia Mounds, the site of one of the most important Native American cities in the days before Columbus came to America.

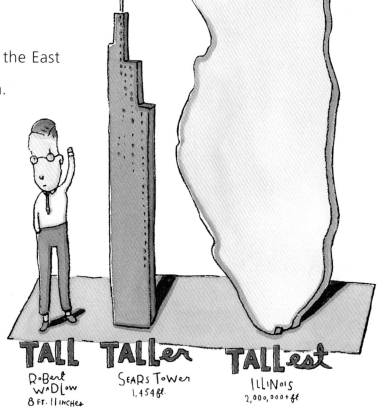

TALL
RoBert WaDLow
8 FT. 11 INCHes

TALLer
SEARs Tower
1,454 ft.

TALLest
ILLINois
2,000,000+ ft

CAHOKIA

pldzn cblpx
drkda pwrn

 A. Residents gave the town its name by randomly picking letters out of a hat! "Aledo" was the first pronounceable name they pieced together.

Wow! Check out the view from atop this hill.

This isn't a hill, J.P. We're on top of Monk's Mound, the largest remaining prehistoric earthwork in North America. It is as tall as a ten-story building with a commanding view of 65 other mounds that were once part of a Native American city that was home to 20,000 people. Native Americans arrived in Illinois about 10,000 years ago. They hunted the animal herds that once covered the United States. Three thousand years ago Native Americans began growing corn, squash and other crops. Southern Illinois became a trading center. Archeologists have found copper from Lake Superior to the north, minerals from Wyoming in the west, and seashells from the Gulf of Mexico to the south.

Native Americans began to build this city off the Mississippi River in about 900 a.d. Using little more than shovels and baskets, people moved more than 22 million cubic feet of earth! It took 300 years to finish Monk's Mound.

Q. Why is southern Illinois called Little Egypt?

That's a lot of dirt!

Yep—enough to make about three million sandcastles. They also built a huge five-story building on top that historians think was probably used as a temple. Many smaller mounds built in different shapes were used as temples, homes and burial grounds. The Native American Indians who lived here used advanced farming methods, were well organized and knew about engineering. They also made wooden sun calendars to keep track of the seasons and schedule ceremonies.

But what happened to all the people?

Nobody knows for sure. They seem to have completely disappeared. It may have been because of disease, wars, droughts or floods. Whatever the reason, by the time Christopher Columbus first landed in America in 1492, Cahokia had been abandoned.

 A. When European pioneers arrived, the region reminded them of what they imagined Egypt looked like. Several places (Cairo, Thebes, Karnak) were given Egyptian names.

Why would Illinois be the center of a Native American civilization?

the MISSISSIPPI RIVER IS LIKE A GIANT HIGHWAY

Because of its rivers. Before cars or airplanes, the easiest way to move long distances was by water. The Mississippi River was like a giant highway with lots of other rivers serving as roads. Today, Illinois' boundaries are largely set by the Mississippi, Ohio and Wabash rivers. The state got its name from the Illinois River, which had first been named after Indians who called themselves the "Illini" (pronounced El-eye-en-eye). When the first French explorers came up the Mississippi River in the late 1600s, they added "-ois" to the name.

Does that mean that Illinois once belonged to France, Lorraine?

Yes. Father Jacques Marquette and explorer Louis Jolliet were the first

Q. How did the Ice Cream Sundae get its name?

Europeans in Illinois. The French built forts and trading outposts all along the Mississippi River to trap and trade fur. France lost control of Illinois in 1763 after a war with England. During the Revolutionary War fifteen years later, American soldiers led by George Rogers Clark captured Illinois. Of course, there wasn't much to take, aside from a few outposts along the rivers. Most of Illinois was still open prairie lands and wilderness. In 1800, there were fewer than 2,500 colonists in all of Illinois.

What about the Indians?

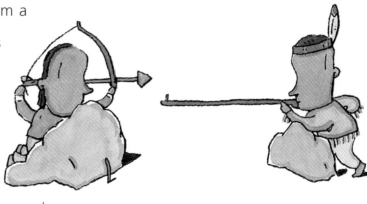

ILLINI

IROQUOIS

They were still here, but they were starting to die off from diseases brought by European settlers. Also, wars broke out as tribes from the east such as the Iroquois were pushed into Illinois. The Iroquois had guns and easily defeated the unarmed Illini tribes.

 It used to be illegal to sell ice cream with flavored soda on Sundays in Evanston, Illinois. Some traders served ice cream with syrup instead, calling it a "Sundae."

W e're now in the Shawnee National Forest, one of the few hilly parts of Illinois and a great place to learn about Illinois' geology.

Geology? That's supposed to be boring—but those strange rocks look kind of neat. What are they?

Those rocks are part of what's called the Garden of the Gods, J.P. Wind and water forged the rocks into spectacular shapes over the last 200 million years. They have names like Camel Rock, Fat Man's Squeeze and the Devil's Smokestack. Unlike the rest of Illinois, glaciers never covered the Shawnee National Forest. Huge sheets of ice and snow, sometimes many miles thick, came down from Canada and covered almost all of Illinois during the course of millions of years, flattening the land as they moved. To the north, they dug deep channels to form the Great Lakes. When the glaciers retreated to the Arctic, they left an enormous layer of fine silt behind. Grasslands grew on top of

the DEVIL'S SMOKESTACK

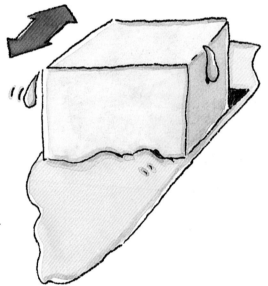

Q. Why are there so many bird houses in the town of Griggsville, Illinois?

the silt. Layer upon layer of decomposed grass piled higher and higher to create a very rich soil. By the time the first settlers arrived, Illinois had some of the most fertile earth in the world.

Wow! That's pretty cool! And what about those caves?

In addition to the unusual rocks, there are lots of interesting caves here. Equality Cave has 2 1/2 miles of passageways, some with ceilings as high as 30 feet. Cave-in-Rock by the Ohio River was once used as a hideout for pirates led by Samuel Mason. Mason etched a sign in front stating "Liquor Vault and House of Entertainment." When people went inside to look, Mason's pirates robbed them.

 Town officials built more than 500 bird nests to attract purple martins during the summer so the migratory bird would eat the local mosquitoes.

It sounds like Illinois was a dangerous place.

It was. The Mississippi River was great for traveling, but it was also treacherous. More than 300 boats sank between Cairo and St. Louis by 1867. Steamboat pilots called that section of the river "the graveyard." The Mississippi is one of the most powerful rivers in the world. When the river swelled from heavy rains, it sometimes changed course and spread into new areas—occasionally flooding farmland and wrecking towns. Kaskaskia was France's most important settlement in Illinois. When white settlers from the United States starting moving to Illinois in the early 1800s, many went

Q. Where can you find the Liberty Bell of the West?

there to farm its fertile fields. In 1818, Illinois became the 21st state in the Union. For two years, Kaskaskia was the state capital. In 1844, the Mississippi River changed course, carving a new route through part of the town, and making the rest an island. An 1881 flood obliterated the island and changed the course of the river again. The name of the town was transferred to a nearby village. Today Kaskaskia is the only part of Illinois on the west side of the Mississippi River.

WHEN the MISSISSIPPI RIVER CHANGED COURSE, IT COULD SWALLOW A WHOLE TOWN

I guess what Mother Nature gives, she can also take.

That's been true in Illinois. Nature has been very good to most Illinois farmers and citizens, but Illinois also suffered the most deadly tornado in the nation's history. On March 18, 1925, a tornado swept across southern Illinois and parts of Missouri and Indiana that killed 695 people. More people have been killed by tornadoes in Illinois than in any other state.

BONG!

 A. In Kaskaskia, Illinois. When Revolutionary soldiers captured the town on July 4, 1778, Americans celebrated by ringing the town bell.

Lorraine, why did they move the capital from Kaskaskia before the floods?

Illinois was changing. People no longer came here to trap furs along the rivers. New settlers swept in from Kentucky and Tennessee on the Ohio River to start farms on the prairie. One of the most important roads of the 1800s, the National Road, was built to help make it easier for settlers to move into Illinois and other states. The road ended at Vandalia, which became the state capital in 1820. Nineteen years later, Springfield, farther north, became the capital.

SPRINGFIELD HERE WE COME!

What was the prairie like in those days?

It was beautiful. High grass covered the flatlands. Stunning flowers, some as

Q. What silly law applies to barber shops in Illinois?

high as a horse's shoulder, graced the landscape. You can still see what the original prairie looked like in a few places, but most of it is now farmland. The soil was so rich, you practically had to jump out of the way when you planted a seed, it grew so fast.

Really?

Well, I'm exaggerating—but not by much. Illinois soil was the most fertile in the world. Still, the first farmers had a big problem. The deep roots of the existing plants and grasses made it almost impossible to cut through the soil. People (and animals) exhausted themselves just to prepare a few acres of land. Plus, farmers kept having to stop plowing to remove the sticky dirt from their plow blades. Finally, in 1837, a blacksmith named John Deere invented a steel plow that "scoured" itself clean as the plow moved forward. He sold ten of his plows in 1839. Fifteen years later, he was selling more than 10,000 plows a year and Illinois prairie was covered by farmland.

 A. A law making it illegal for barbers to use their fingers to put shaving cream on a customer's face!

Even with the Deere plow, life on the prairie was hard. Fires often tore through the high grasses, engulfing farms in flames. So many people got malaria, a deadly disease that gives people the shivers (among other symptoms), that the malady became known as "the Illinois shakes." But the hard-working farmers prevailed. Today, 80 percent of the state is covered by farms.

Is that why Illinois is called the "Garden Spot of the Nation?"

That's right, J.P. Most of Illinois is like a giant flat tabletop covered with a patchwork of farms. About 1 million people work on more than 70,000 farms or for companies that process Illinois farm products. Illinois exports more farm products than any other state in the nation. Corn is the most important Illinois crop. Each year Illinois farmers grow about 200 billion ears of corn, most of which are used to feed livestock. McLean County produces more corn than any

Q. Who was the tallest man in the world?

other county in the nation, and corn festivals sweep through the state each September to celebrate the harvests. Illinois grows more soybeans and raises more hogs than any other state except Iowa. Most soybeans are used as animal feed, but they are also used to make margarine, tofu, cooking oils and soy sauce. Champaign County grows more soybeans than any other county. The city of Decatur is known as the soybean capital of the world. Other farms grow wheat, oats, alfalfa, hay, fruits and vegetables, or raise cattle, sheep and chickens. Illinois chicken farmers sell about 800 million eggs a year. All of which is why Chicago later became one of the most important cities in the world, but we'll get to that later.

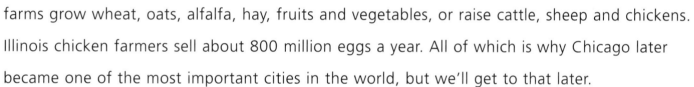

Didn't Abraham Lincoln work on a farm, Lorraine?

Yes. He grew up on farms in Kentucky, where he was born, and in Indiana, where he spent his boyhood.

 A. Robert Wadlow of Alton, Illinois. He grew to 8 feet and 11 inches. Wadlow died in 1940 at the age of 22 from an infected foot blister.

I want to know more about Lincoln.

Let's go to New Salem. Lincoln moved here in 1831 when he was 22 years old. Like the other settlers, he hoped to cash in on trade passing down the Sangamon River, which was a typical Illinois frontier town. When Lincoln arrived there were only 12 families living in New Salem, each with a log cabin they called home. Unfortunately, the river trade passed over New Salem. Six years later, it was abandoned. New Salem would have been lost to history, like most unsuccessful frontier towns, if it weren't for Lincoln's residence there. The state has restored New Salem with authentic log cabins and historical exhibits.

Let's go look!

Well, the log cabins are all pretty much the same, J.P., with uncomfortable chairs, dirt floors, and chamber pots. Living in a log cabin,

LINCOLN the RIVER TRADER

Q. What was Lincoln's job before he entered politics?

breaking sod to start a farm and trying to make a living in the backwoods was hard work. Lincoln wrote that he was raised with an axe in his hand and hardly set it down until he was a man. When Lincoln packed his cases and moved to Springfield, he was happy to put it behind him.

By that time, the last Native Americans had been pushed out of Illinois. In 1832, an Indian chief named Black Hawk waged a last desperate war against white settlers. But the U.S. Army and Illinois volunteers (including Lincoln) defeated the 1,000-warrior army. After 150 years of off-and-on battles with Native Americans, Illinois' pioneers could concentrate on building their state.

 A. He worked as a surveyor, store clerk, boatman on the Mississippi River, farmhand, and was even postmaster of New Salem. And in his spare time, Lincoln taught himself grammar and law!

Springfield has been the capital of Illinois since 1839. Its imposing capitol building looms large with a dome 403 feet high, or the same height as a 40-story building.

There sure are a lot of historic sites about Lincoln here, Lorraine!

Yep. This is where Lincoln became a successful lawyer and politician. "To this place, and the kindness of these people, I owe everything," Lincoln said of Springfield when he left for Washington D.C. to serve as President in 1861. The only home Lincoln owned is here. You can visit Lincoln's law office and see where he gave his famous "House Divided" speech at the Old State Capitol. You can even visit his family pew at the First Presbyterian Church. Lincoln is buried in Springfield. They say that if you touch the nose of the bronze head of Lincoln outside the tomb entrance, it brings you good luck.

Q. Were there slaves in Illinois?

What was the "House Divided" speech?

Only one of the most famous speeches in American history, J.P.! In 1858, Lincoln ran for the U.S. Senate against a man named Stephen A. Douglas. Lincoln did not believe that the United States should allow slavery to spread to new states. Douglas believed new states should decide for themselves whether to permit the slave trade. The two men held debates all over Illinois that were reported in newspapers across the country. Lincoln said, "A house

divided by itself cannot stand. I believe this government cannot endure permanently half slave and half free." Although Douglas won the election, Lincoln became famous for his stand against slavery. In 1860, he was elected President. Fearing that Lincoln would end slavery in the South, 11 southern states tried to leave the Union. Lincoln refused to let them and the Civil War started.

 Slavery was abolished in Illinois in 1848, but that did not mean blacks were welcome. For several years it was illegal for an African American to live here.

Four score and seven years ago....
*87 Years

THE GETTYSBURG ADDRESS

Lincoln led the nation through the Civil War. It was a terrible and difficult time. Despite repeated military defeats, Lincoln pushed the war forward in order to keep the country united. His speech at Gettysburg and his Second Inaugural Address are among the most important speeches in American history. Lincoln became known as the Great Emancipator for emancipating the slaves, or setting them free. But victory came at a terrible price. More than 600,000 Americans were killed in the war, and a few days after the war ended, Lincoln was assassinated.

Was there any fighting in Illinois?

Very little. But more than 250,000 soldiers from Illinois served in the war, and 35,000 were killed. The man remembered as the North's

Q. When was the first Memorial Day celebrated?

greatest general, Ulysses S. Grant, came from the Illinois town of Galena. Grant led the North to victory in some of the most important battles of the war. He was hailed as a national hero after the war, and was elected President in 1868 and 1872. Unfortunately, though he was a great general, he is considered one of the worst presidents in U.S. history. Many of the people he appointed to important positions stole money from the government.

ULYSSeα S. GRANT

Did Grant steal money?

No, he didn't, J.P. He was a very good and honest man. When he married his wife, he freed a slave given to him by his father-in-law, even though he was broke. As President, Grant helped give important rights to emancipated slaves in the South to help them become a part of free society. But Grant let his friends take advantage of him and he was reluctant to stop them.

A. On April 29, 1866, the people of Carbondale, Illinois, held the first Memorial Day service in honor of those who died in the Civil War. It is now a national holiday held on the fourth Monday in May.

What about Chicago, Lorraine?
I want to check that place out!

We're getting there, J.P—only a few more stops first. Don't forget that Chicago became big and important only because of what was happening in the rest of Illinois and the Midwest. Around the time of the Civil War, Chicago became the region's commercial and trading center. Canals and railroads converged at Chicago, but they stretched all throughout the Illinois farm country.

New inventions made it easier for farmers to grow more crops and raise more livestock. A mechanical reaper invented by an Illinois man named Cyrus McCormick saved time and labor in harvesting crops. In 1873, Joseph Gidden began manufacturing barbed wire. The invention changed farming across the nation. Instead of growing hedges or building expensive split-rail fences, farmers could separate fields with cheap barbed-wire fences—"horse high, hog tight, and bull strong"—to keep livestock from wandering off. And at the turn of the century, the Caterpillar company began building tractors that revolutionized farming.

Q. What city is known as the barbed-wire capital of the world?

Why was it named Caterpillar?

Because instead of wheels, the first tractors used tracks like those on a tank. Somebody said they looked like caterpillars, and the name stuck. The company got its start in California, but moved to Peoria, Illinois, where it became the world's largest heavy-equipment manufacturer.

Illinois' central location and the construction of a huge transportation system made it easier for the state's farms and agricultural industry to sell their products to distant markets. It is still that way today. Chicago has the largest rail center in the country. More than 65 million people travel each year through Chicago's O'Hare International Airport, one of the world's busiest airports.

BUSY O'HARE AIRPORT

There are more than 2,000 miles of interstate highways. The Illinois and Mississippi rivers allow companies to haul coal, heavy machines, grain and other products by barge to the Gulf of Mexico. Ships can go directly across the Great Lakes to the Atlantic Ocean.

 DeKalb, Illinois, where the first barbed wire was manufactured.

29

Back up for a second, Lorraine! Didn't you say African Americans were not even allowed to live in Illinois before the Civil War? When did your family arrive?

In the early 1900s thousands of African Americans moved out of the South to northern states such as Illinois in search of jobs at factories. My great-grandparents believed they would find better opportunities here than in the South. They did find work, but many whites were still prejudiced against blacks, and some thought black people would take away their jobs. Race riots (in this case, violent disputes between blacks and whites) erupted. In 1917, more than 100 African Americans were killed in two riots at East St. Louis. Two years later, a six-day riot in Chicago resulted in the deaths of 23 blacks and 16 whites. Just because the laws were different in the North, didn't mean there weren't problems.

EARLY 20th CENTURY RIOTS

Q. How fast can a white-tailed deer run?

But didn't things get better?

Slowly, J.P., and the process continues today. I'm named after a famous black woman, Lorraine Hansberry, who was born in 1930 and wrote a play called *A Raisin in the Sun* in 1959, about racism in Chicago. Hansberry was the youngest American, the first woman, and the first African American to win the New York Drama Critics Circle Award for Best Play. That's a big deal! The story is about an African-American family who remain united as they struggle against racism and poverty. Hansberry grew up in a middle-class African-American family in Chicago, just like mine.

A RAISIN IN the SUN

When her family moved to a white neighborhood, a mob gathered and threw bricks, one of which almost hit her. She was eight years old at the time. This event, and experiences like it, inspired her to write the award-winning play.

WAIT UP!

 A. Up to 40 miles per hour! They love the open plains and can be found throughout Illinois.

Hey, look at that eagle!
And there goes a buffalo!

This is Wildlife Prairie Park, located ten miles outside of Preoria. A sister park to the Brookfield Zoo in Chicago, it is one of the country's premier wildlife parks. It shows off 2,000 acres of prairie, and it looks similar to the way most of Illinois looked 200 years ago. A cross between a theme park and a conservation exhibit, it holds more than 70 endangered animals and 300 endangered plants. Bison, elk, bears, cougars, wolves, badgers, bobcats, wild turkeys, opossums, sandhill cranes, skunks, woodchucks, beavers, river otters, and almost every other historic species from pioneer days all have a home here.

It's as if my science class came alive, Lorraine! What about birds in Illinois?

Q. What's special about the McDonald's restaurant at Fox Lake, Illinois?

WE SHOULD HAVE TAKEN A Left IN CLEVELAND...

Millions of birds migrate through Illinois each spring and every fall along the Mississippi River. As many as two million wild ducks fly to the Illinois Valley. Geese from Canada flock by the thousands to the Shawnee Hills each winter. Game birds such as pheasants and quail abound throughout the state. In the forests of southern Illinois, you can find great blue heron, wild turkey and many songbirds, including the state bird, the cardinal.

How about elephants?

Only in zoos and circuses. A 6,500-pound circus elephant named Norma Jean was buried in the Oquawka town square—near the spot where she was struck dead by a bold of lightning in 1972. Her trainer was thrown 30 feet into the air. Town residents commemorate Norma Jean's shocking death with a festival each August. It includes bake sales featuring elephant ears, a white elephant sale, and an elephant walk.

A. It's the only one in the world with drive-up service for boats!

Are there any other odd places like that in Illinois?

At Gays, Illinois, stands the world's only two-story outhouse (a toilet without water or plumbing). It was built in the 1880s for some second-story apartments above a general store that was torn down years ago. Residents call it a "skyscrapper." I think it's gross.

Me too!

Then there's the Oliver Parks Telephone Museum in Telephone, Illinois, with more than 100 antique phones on display. But don't bother calling them. They don't have a working phone in the place. Up in Dixon, you can visit the Ronald Reagan Boyhood Home. Despite Lincoln's fame, Reagan is the only U.S. president actually born in Illinois. The Nashua Hotel in Dixon, however, has

Q. What's a "dead man's hand"?

hosted five presidents (Lincoln, Grant, Theodore Roosevelt, Howard Taft and Reagan). At Hanover, we can visit Whistling Wings, the largest mallard duck hatchery in the world. More than 200,000 ducks are hatched every year.

Better keep Maggie out of there—she loves to chase birds!

Finally, there is Galena in northern Illinois. Galena burst onto the American frontier in the 1820s as a lead-mining town. When Chicago was a quiet trading post on Lake Michigan with barely enough people for a baseball game, Galena bustled with riverboat traffic and 15,000 residents. Today, Galena is one of the best-preserved historic towns in the nation. Nearly 85 percent of the town has been designated as a historic district. The skyline looks pretty much the same way it did at the outset of the Civil War when Grant ran a family leather goods store there. Today, Galena's Main Street overflows with boutiques, craft shops and art galleries.

Speaking of Chicago....

Alright, J.P. We're heading there now.

A. It's a poker term for a hand of aces and eights. The famed Western lawman "Wild Bill" Hickok of Troy Grove, Illinois, was shot in the back while holding that hand in a poker game.

At last! Chicago!
Hog Butcher for the World,
Tool Maker, Stacker of Wheat,
Player with Railroads and the Nation's
Freight Handler; Stormy, husky,
brawling, City of the Big Shoulders.

Hey, you're stealing my lines—or at least the lines of poet Carl Sandburg, who was born in Galesburg, Illinois, in 1878. Sandburg spent much of his life in the state. He worked as a reporter for the *Chicago Daily News* and wrote a famous book of poetry called *Chicago Poems.*

Chicago is the third largest city in the United States, behind New York and Los Angeles. Located in the heart of the Midwest, many people pass through as they travel from one part of the country to another. With its soaring skyscrapers, vigorous industry, windy avenues and hearty people, Chicago leaves visitors awestruck. It is a big city with big buildings and big accomplishments. "I reel, I sway, I am utterly exhausted," Ogden Nash wrote of Chicago.

Q. Which famous British poet didn't care for Chicago?

But it wasn't always so. Chicago started out as a remote trading post founded in 1779 by a Haitian fur trader named Jean Baptiste Pointe du Sable on Lake Michigan's shore. The U.S. army later built a small military garrison here called Fort Dearborn. Its only claim to fame for the next 50 years was a terrible Indian massacre at the outset of the War of 1812 in which 53 of 100 soldiers, women and children were killed, and the fort was burned to the ground. Rebuilt in 1816, the area remained a swampy backwater. When the Illinois survey was conducted in 1830, Chicago's population totaled 50 people.

How many people are there today?

Nearly three million—more than 20 times the population of the next largest city in Illinois.

A. Rudyard Kipling. "Having seen it, I urgently desire never to see it again," he wrote.

Canals and railroads made Chicago what it is, J.P. The government decided in 1830 to build a canal from the Illinois River to Lake Michigan at Chicago. This meant that ships could carry freight from New York City up the Hudson River, across the Erie Canal, through the Great Lakes, down the Mississippi River—and Chicago was the linchpin. Speculators swooped into Chicago to buy land, pushing the price from $100 a lot in 1830 to $100,000 in 1836. But it took longer than expected to finish the canal, and prices eventually collapsed back to $100.

Wow! Somebody must have lost a lot of money.

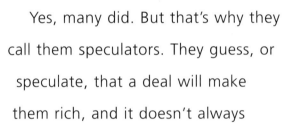

Yes, many did. But that's why they call them speculators. They guess, or speculate, that a deal will make them rich, and it doesn't always work. In 1848, workers finished the Illinois & Michigan Canal, and more importantly, the first railroad line into Chicago was completed. Chicago had at last become a

Q. What building produces some of the yummiest aromas in Chicago?

commercial hub for farmers and ranchers, who could now move their crops and livestock to places far outside the Midwest. The population in Chicago soared from 28,000 in 1850 to 110,000 in 1860 and 300,000 in 1870. By 1890, Chicago's 1.1 million residents made it the second largest city in the nation. It wasn't just people who moved to Chicago. Thousands of sheep, cattle and pigs came to market in Chicago. Chicago's stockyards could hold 20,000 cattle, 75,000 hogs, and 20,000 sheep at a time.

It must have stunk!

It did. Some people called Chicago "Porkopolis." So many pigs went to Chicago slaughterhouses in one year that if you lined them up head-to-tail in single file they would stretch all the way to New York City. Chicago's capacity to butcher pigs was legendary. Meatpacking baron Gustavus Swift bragged, "We use everything but the squeal."

 The world's largest cookie and cracker factory! Among other goodies, Nabisco bakes 16 billion Oreo cookies a year there.

Despite all of its success, J.P., Chicago grew a little too fast for its own good. The city was crowded with mud and filth. Most of the buildings were wooden, cheap and in very close quarters. Then, disaster struck on October 8, 1871. According to legend, a cow owned by Mrs. Catherine O'Leary kicked over a lantern that ignited some hay. The barn caught fire. Flames quickly swept through the city.

Nearly 20,000 buildings were destroyed, 300 people were killed, and more than 100,000 people became homeless. Flying ashes from Chicago sparked forest fires as far away as Michigan and Wisconsin.

Why didn't that put an end to Chicago's growth?

Chicago was still in the center of one of the fastest growing, wealthiest regions in the world at the time. In fact, the fire allowed Chicago to start over and rebuild the city in a more sensible, modern way. The world's first "skyscraper" was built in Chicago—

Q. Why is Chicago called "the Windy City"?

the 10-story Home Insurance Building—in 1885. Many more steel-structure skyscrapers followed. Chicago became the world's capital of architecture, a position it still holds.

How could Chicago afford to build skyscrapers? It couldn't just have been from pigs and sheep.

Industry flourished in Chicago. It became the leading manufacturer of steel rails, railroad cars, and farm machinery. Because of the transportation routes from Chicago, the first mail-order business was started there. It is all still important today. Look at the incredible Sears Tower, built with money from the famous mail-order company. When it was completed in 1974, it was the tallest building in the world (though taller skyscrapers have since been built). The $300 million building reaches 1,454 feet into the air.

A. Chicago got its nickname from a New York City newspaper editor who got tired of hearing people from Chicago boast. He thought they were "windy," or full of hot air.

41

Chicago must have been an exciting place!

Well, J.P., it was and it wasn't. Chicago still had terrible slums. Immigrants and poor people lived in dreadful conditions. Unlike today, there were no day-care centers for kids and very little government support for the poor, the sick or the elderly. Conditions were so bad that garbage was left strewn in the street by city garbage collectors and, in some especially awful cases, children were even tied to their beds while their parents went to work in factories!

In 1889, a young woman named Jane Addams opened Hull House. Addams started programs such as a center for child care, a library, classes for learning to read, free legal services for the poor, a working girls' home and a boys' club. Addams provided visiting nurses to assist families in their homes. Many people came to Hull House for weekly baths. Addams waged campaigns against corrupt city officials, and she and her associates are credited with creating the social work profession. Addams became the first American woman to win the Nobel Peace Prize.

Q. How many books does the Chicago Public Library have?

What about the famous Chicago gangsters I've heard about?

Corruption and vice ran so rampant that Chicago was once known as "the wickedest city in the country." Chicago reached its low point in the 1920s when criminals like Al Capone waged gang wars to control the illegal liquor business. Capone was very charming and liked to talk to newspaper reporters. He became the world's most famous gangster. But Capone was a killer who earned his nickname "Scarface" from a wound he suffered in a knife fight. One of his most notorious crimes was the "St. Valentine's Day Massacre," which he ordered in 1929. That's when, on Valentine's Day, his henchmen wiped out an opposing gang in a hail of bullets. Eventually Capone went to jail for—of all things—not paying taxes.

 Two million! It's the world's largest public library.

What about Chicago today?

It's a great place to visit, especially for kids like us, J.P. Lincoln Park is one of the country's premier city parks. More than five miles long, with beaches stretching along Lake Michigan, its bike paths, ball fields and the great Lincoln Park Zoo—you've got to see the gorillas there—attract millions of people every year. Even though Chicago is in the middle of the continent, it has a beach!

The city is located on the shores of Lake Michigan, which is the largest lake contained entirely within the US borders. Lake Michigan is more than 300 miles long, 118 miles wide and nearly 900 feet deep, giving it waves similar to the ocean. A lot of people in Chicago go boating on it.

There are also great museums in Chicago, like the Museum of Science and Industry. A full-size replica of an Illinois coal mine, a World War II submarine, and a giant dollhouse that cost almost half a million dollars to build are just a few of the 2,000 exhibits there. The Art Institute of Chicago has works by some of the world's greatest painters.

Q. Chicago has seen some famous firsts. What about famous lasts?

Then there's Chicago's great music! Louis Armstrong, Benny Goodman and Miles Davis helped bring jazz to Chicago, setting a standard of excellence that still stands. The country's most famous comedy club, Second City, is in Chicago. Great comedians like Bill Murray, John Belushi, John Candy and Joan Rivers are just a few of the stars who performed there.

Why "Second City," Lorraine?

People started calling Chicago the Second City when it was rebuilt after the 1871 fire. But Chicago has hosted a lot of firsts since then. The world's first Ferris wheel was built at Chicago's 1893 World's Columbian Exposition. The first automobile race was held from Chicago to Evanston in 1905. (The winner drove at an average speed of $7\frac{1}{2}$ miles per hour.) The first air-conditioned movie theater opened in Chicago in 1919.

 Wrigley Field, home of the Chicago Cubs, was the last Major League baseball stadium to install lights.

Our trip is coming to an end.

Well, I'm sad that we're nearly through,
but Maggie and I sure have enjoyed it.
We've seen so much I can hardly remember it all!

Remember this about Illinois, J.P.: It is the people that made this a great state. Coming from all corners of the world, whether it was Asian rice fields, Polish villages or a sharecropper's shanty in the South, they have learned to live together and build a great state.

Chicago was the center of the Civil Rights Movement of the 1960s—when people fought for fair treatment of African Americans—and it has been an important political center ever since. We've had world-class gangsters and winners of the Nobel Peace Prize, crooked city politicians and the greatest president (Abraham Lincoln) in our nation's history, some of the world's best architects and the worst city slums in history. Illinois' citizens include the great conservative President Ronald Reagan and some of

Q. What did the Indian word "Illini" mean?

the most eloquent liberal voices of the 20th century, such as the Democratic Governor Adlai Stevenson, feminist writer Betty Friedan, and black civil rights leader the Rev. Jesse Jackson.

That's a lot of different kinds of people!

It sure is, and it's that diversity that made our country great. We can be afraid of our differences or we can embrace them. Residents of Illinois didn't always welcome people of different backgrounds, colors or religions at first, but we have learned to live together. A black man named Jean Baptiste Pointe du Sable founded what would become Chicago. Gritty pioneers conquered the prairies, and produce from their farms turned Chicago into one of the world's greatest cities. Whether it's farmers, factory workers or fighters for equal rights for everyone, Illinois has produced some amazing Americans.

It sure has, Lorraine. Thanks for showing us so much. Maggie and I have learned a lot!

A. The people.

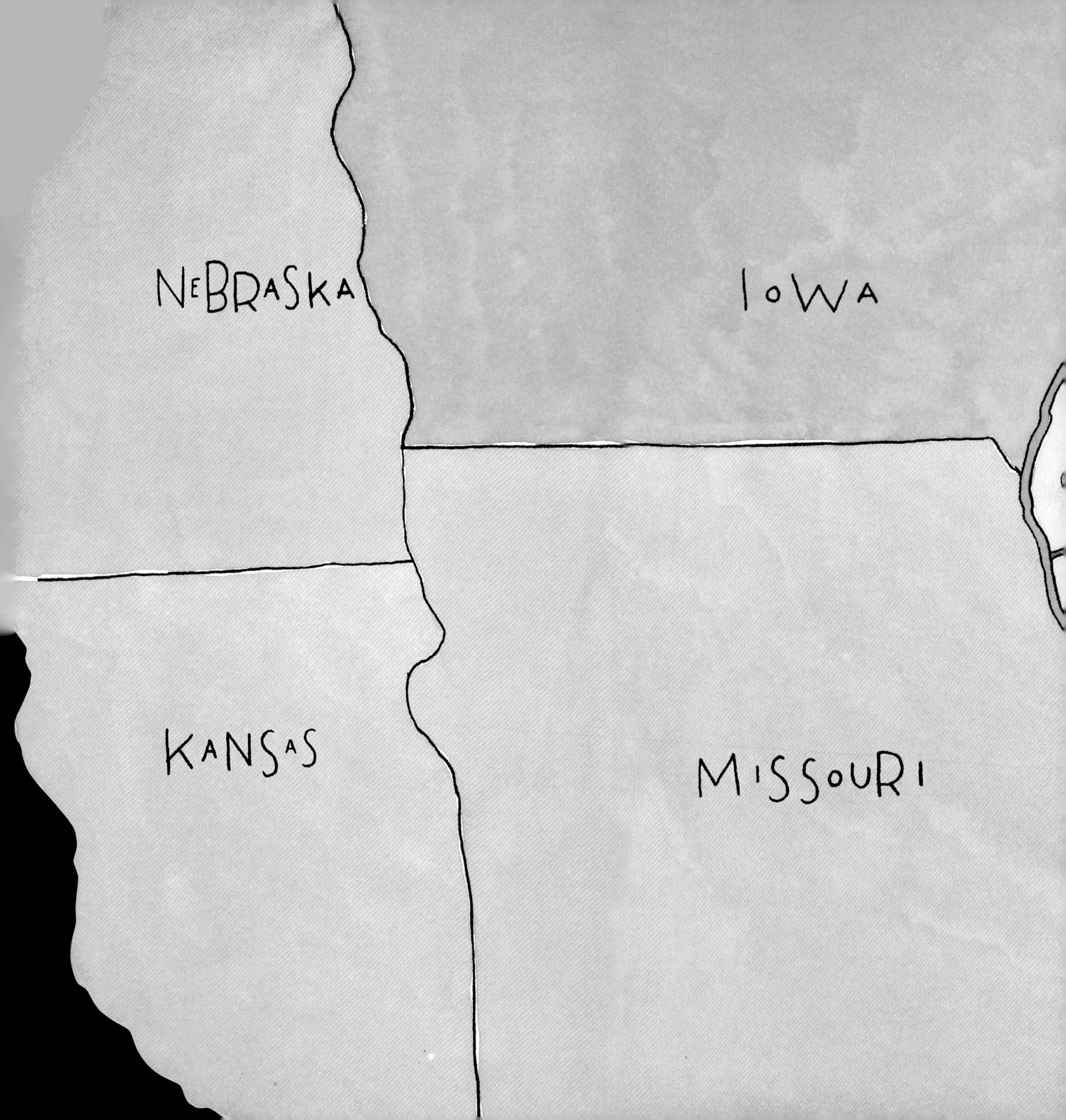
NEBRASKA
IOWA
KANSAS
MISSOURI

STATE SHAPES